Read All About Sharks

# DIVING WITH SHARKS

## Lynn Stone

The Rourke Corporation, Inc.
Vero Beach, Florida 32964

PHOTO CREDITS
©Tom Campbell: cover, p.22; ©David B. Fleetham/INNERSPACE VISIONS: p.4; ©Bob Friel/INNERSPACE VISIONS: p.6; ©Marty Snyderman: p.7, 9, 12, 16, 18, 19, 20; ©Herb Segars: p.10; ©James D. Watt/INNERSPACE VISIONS: p.13; ©Ron and Valerie Taylor/INNERSPACE VISIONS: p.15

**Library of Congress Cataloging-in-Publication Data**

Stone, Lynn M.
    Diving with sharks / by Lynn M. Stone.
        p. cm. — (Read all about sharks)
    Includes index.
    Summary: Describes what it is like to see sharks in their natural environment and discusses dangers that divers face and how they protect themselves.
    ISBN 0-86593-442-8 (alk. paper)
    1. Sharks—Juvenile literature. 2. Scuba diving—Juvenile literature.
[1. Sharks. 2. Scuba diving.]
I. Title II. Series: Stone, Lynn M. Read all about sharks
QL638.9.S846 1996
597'.31—dc20                                           96–7966
                                                        CIP
                                                        AC

**Printed in the USA**

# TABLE OF CONTENTS

# DIVING WITH SHARKS

Seeing a shark undersea is "one diver's **nightmare** (NITE mair) and another's dream come true," says Marty Snyderman.

For him, seeing sharks close up in the wild is a dream. He is one of a small group of people who dive just to find sharks. Mr. Snyderman took several of the photos in this book.

Many undersea divers, however, don't really *want* to see sharks. Sharks are both the biggest and most dangerous fish on earth.

*Diving with sharks puts divers up-close with some of the largest and most dangerous fish in the world.*

# SHARING THE SEA WITH SHARKS

The shark's **habitat** (HAB uh tat), or home, is the ocean. Sharks live and swim easily undersea. The sea is a challenge for people. Diving requires special equipment—a diving suit, fins, mask, **oxygen tank** (OX uh jin TANK), and more.

*A diver feeds a gray reef shark by hand.*

*A blue shark swims past a diver holding baitfish.*

Divers who seek sharks take on a special challenge. They watch, study, and even feed sharks in the shark's own neighborhood.

For these divers, briefly sharing the sea with sharks is a treat. Shark divers enjoy the power, beauty, and gracefulness of sharks up-close.

## SHARK CHILLS

Sunshine can't reach deep into the sea. Undersea light is dim. A diver can't see far in any direction. Sea creatures suddenly appear and disappear.

"It gives me a chill," says Mr. Snyderman, "to watch sharks appear from nowhere and swim right in my direction."

Imagine a 15-foot shark that weighs more than 3,000 pounds almost in your face. "Sheer power," says Snyderman of the shark, "brute force, plain and simple. It's a thrill."

*Divers see the gracefulness—and power—of sharks at arm's reach. Shark photographers like to be within six feet of their subjects!*

# SHARK DIVE!

Divers find sharks in many parts of the world's oceans. Diving companies lead divers to sharks in some places like Spencer Gulf in South Australia, Papua New Guinea, Northern California, and the Bahamas.

Divers find different kinds of sharks at different water depths. Divers don't usually plunge deeper than 135 feet for sharks.

A diver may stay "down"—under water—for as long as an hour. The time, though, depends upon how deep the diver goes.

*Diving companies lead shark-diving trips in areas where sharks are common.*

## SHARK CAGES

Divers often view sharks from a lightweight steel cage. The cage is dropped into the sea from a line on a boat.

The divers inside the cage won't attract sharks, but they release fish as bait. Sharks smell the fish meat and blood. Then they swim toward the cage for food.

*A great white shark, taking a baited line, slams into a steel divers' cage.*

*Curious, a great white shark inspects a diving cage and the divers inside.*

Sharks become fierce and excited with food all around them. During this "feeding **frenzy**" (FREN zee), the divers' cage protects divers from being mistaken as shark food.

# UNDERSEA SAFETY

Divers who work outside of cages do face a small risk of being bitten by a shark. After all, the sea is the shark's home.

Divers who spear fish are warned that bleeding fish may attract sharks. Sharks have a great sense of smell. They also can sense tiny vibrations, like those made by injured fish.

Divers are warned not to swim alone or in places where sharks feed on seals.

*Steel bars of diving cages prevent this great white shark from moving any closer to divers.*

# PROTECTION FROM ATTACK

Most victims of shark attacks, which happen very rarely, are not torn apart by the shark. The victim usually suffers bites and a major loss of blood.

Steel shark suits were designed to prevent bites. The Neptunic shark suit is made of about 400,000 chain links. It weighs about 17 pounds and costs about $8,000.

The suit will protect a diver from the jaws of most sharks, but not from the largest.

Some divers carry an underwater gun, called a bang stick, for protection.

*A shark diver models a stainless steel diving suit.*

# SWIMMING WITH A SHARK

Divers say that swimming with a whale shark, the largest kind of fish in the sea, is a real thrill. The whale shark can be six or seven times longer than a diver. That's about the size of a humpback whale.

*In a thrilling encounter with the world's largest kind of fish, a diver tags along with a giant whale shark.*

*Unprotected, this diver and Marty Snyderman, who took the photo, bravely watch a great white shark.*

Whale sharks eat **plankton** (PLANK ton), the name of a variety of tiny, floating plants and animals. Despite their giant size, whale sharks are quite tame. Sometimes divers hang onto a shark's fins and go along for a ride in the Gulf of Mexico.

# PHOTOGRAPHING SHARKS

Photographing sharks in their habitat requires a great deal of skill—and courage. For sharp photos, a diver needs to be within eight feet of the shark!

Underwater photos require a special waterproof camera. They also require an undersea flash to light up the shark.

Photographers lure some species of sharks up-close with bait. The great white, for example, swims to bait. Photographers cannot bait the big plankton-eating sharks, like the whale and basking.

*Undersea shark photography means using waterproof camera gear and being close to the shark.*

# GLOSSARY

**frenzy** (FREN zee) — a state of great excitement

**habitat** (HAB uh tat) — the special kind of place where an animal lives, such as an ocean coral reef

**nightmare** (NITE mair) — a very frightening dream

**oxygen tank** (OX uh jin TANK) —a container from which undersea divers breathe fresh air

**plankton** (PLANK ton) — tiny, floating plants and animals of the sea and other bodies of water

*Divers at the surface swim with a feeding whale shark. Because whale sharks eat plankton, they are not a threat to divers.*

# INDEX